Thank you for your purchase! If you enjoy this book, please help us with an honest review.

———————— ★★★★ ————————

All rights reserved. No part of this book may be reproduced, stored in any retrieval system, or transmitted in any form or by any means, mechanical, photocopying, recording, or otherwise, without the prior permission of the author.

Cursive handwriting workbook

PART 1. Writing letters in cursive

PART 2. Writing words in cursive

PART 3. Writing sentences in cursive

PART 1

Write letters in cursive

What to do in Part 1?

- Trace the alphabet
- Color the drawing
- Trace the lowercase and the uppercase letter
- Enjoy it!

Cursive Alphabet

Aa Bb Cc Dd Ee
Ff Gg Hh Ii Jj
Kk Ll Mm Nn
Oo Pp Qq Rr Ss
Tt Uu Vv Ww
Xx Yy Zz

Cursive Alphabet

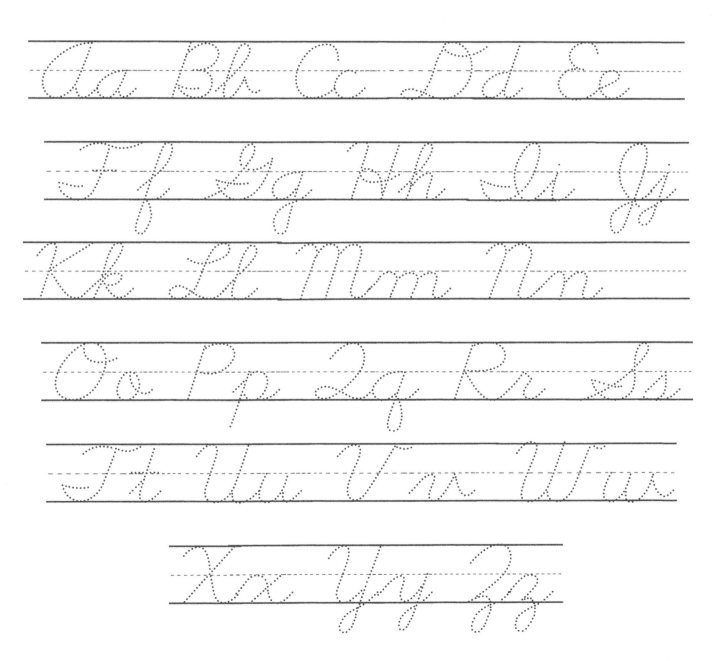

A is for Alligator

D is for Dinosaur

G is for Grapes

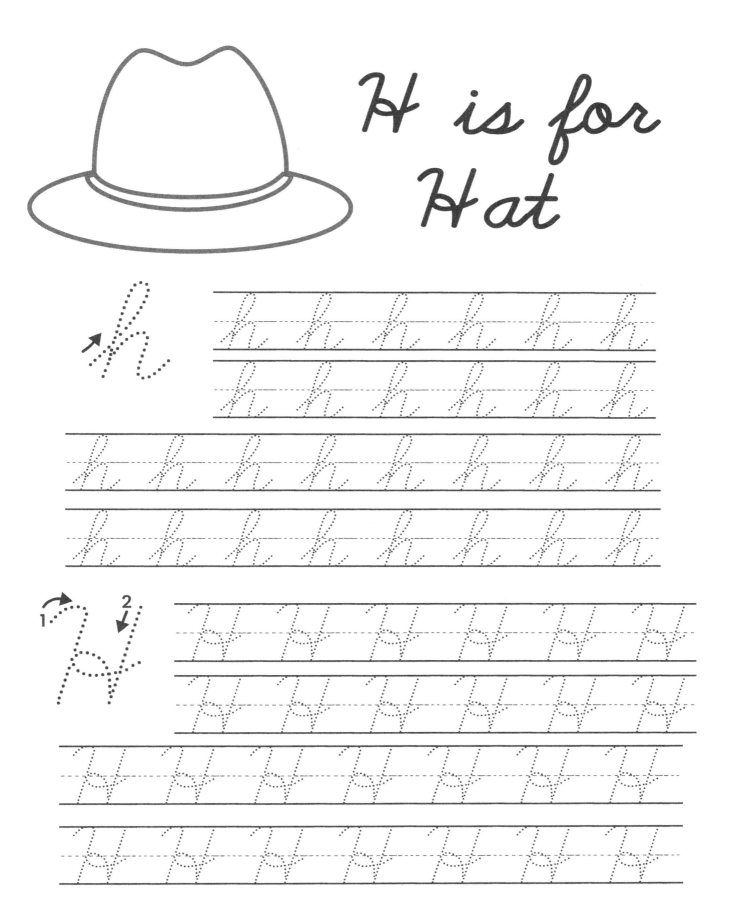

I is for Island

L is for Lion

M is for Monkey

N is for Nest

O is for Octopus

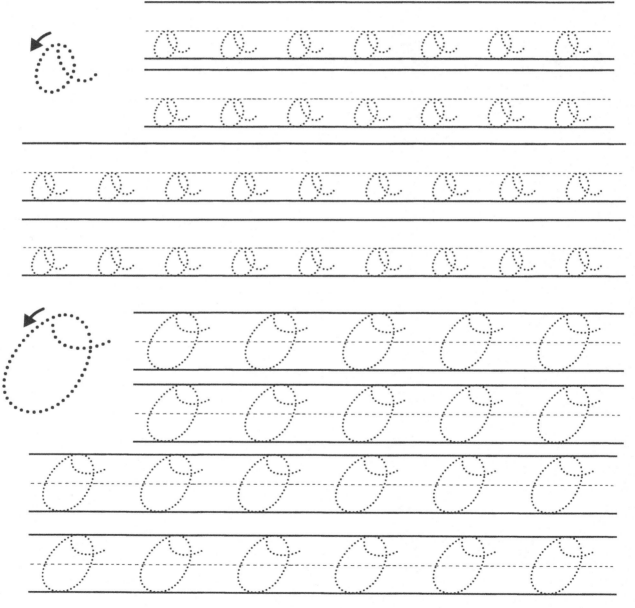

P is for Penguin

2 is for Queen

R is for Rabbit

T is for Turtle

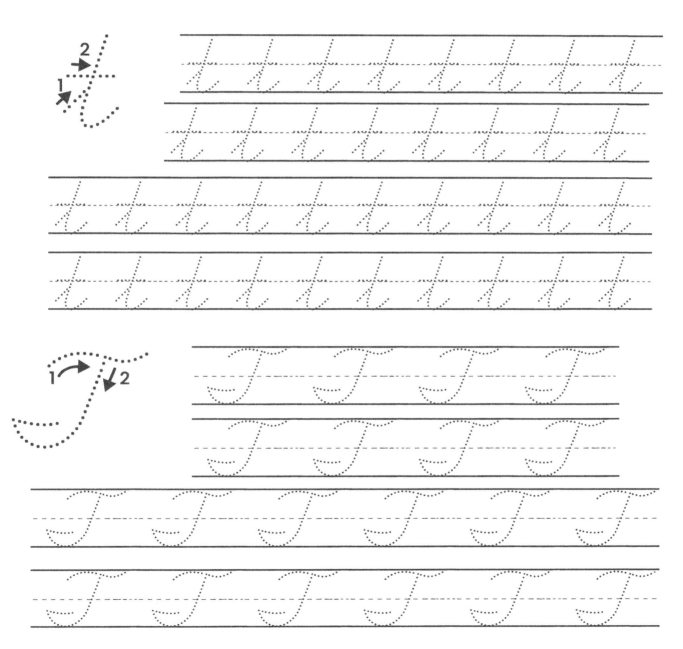

U is for Umbrella

V is for Volcano

W is for Whale

Y is for Yoga

Z is for Zebra

PART 2

Write words in cursive

What to do in Part 2 ?

- Trace the words in each letter
- Write again the words by yourself
- Enjoy it!

Words with A

Ant Ant Ant Ant Ant

Rabbit Rabbit Rabbit

Banana Banana Banana

Apple Apple Apple Apple

Balloon Balloon Balloon

Words with A

a

R

B

a

B

Words with B

Bed Bed Bed Bed Bed Bed

blue blue blue blue blue

Crab Crab Crab Crab Crab

Cub Cub Cub Cub Cub Cub

Ribbon Ribbon Ribbon

Words with B

B

b

C

c

R

Words with C

Words with C

l

c

p

c

k

Words with D

Diamond Diamond

red red red red red red red

candle candle candle

Doll Doll Doll Doll

meadow meadow meadow

Words with D

D

n

c

D

m

Words with E

Eagle Eagle Eagle Eagle

exercise exercise exercise

egg egg egg egg egg egg egg

elephant elephant elephant

eleven eleven eleven

11

Words with E

11

Words with F

Floor Floor Floor Floor

fire fire fire fire fire fire

frog frog frog frog frog frog

coffee coffee coffee coffee

fall fall fall fall fall fall

Words with F

Words with G

Giraffe Giraffe Giraffe

magic magic magic magic

gingerbread gingerbread

Gold Gold Gold Gold Gold

glue glue glue glue glue glue

Words with G

Words with H

Hug Hug Hug Hug Hug Hug Hug

heart heart heart heart

she she she she she she she

hockey hockey hockey hockey

Hen Hen Hen Hen Hen

Words with H

Words with I

Island Island Island

igloo igloo igloo igloo igloo

nice nice nice nice nice nice

pink pink pink pink pink

kid kid kid kid kid kid

Words with I

l

i

n

p

k

Words with J

Jewelery Jewelery Jewelery

jar jar jar jar jar jar jar

project project project project

injection injection injection

jungle jungle jungle jungle

Words with J

Words with K

Koala Koala Koala Koala

joke joke joke joke joke joke

kiss kiss kiss kiss kiss kiss

kitten kitten kitten kitten

skirt skirt skirt skirt

Words with K

K

j

k

k

l

Words with L

Lemon Lemon Lemon

milk milk milk milk milk

castle castle castle castle

Love Love Love Love

plug plug plug plug plug

Words with L

l

m

c

l

p

Words with M

man man man man man

Moon Moon Moon Moon

music music music music

hammer hammer hammer

number number number

Words with M

m

M

m

h

m

Words with N

neck neck neck neck neck

Nose Nose Nose Nose Nose

night night night night

snail snail snail snail

Nine Nine Nine Nine Nine

Words with n

n

n

n

n

n

Words with O

owl owl owl owl owl

Old Old Old Old Old Old

nose nose nose nose nose nose

ocean ocean ocean ocean

orange orange orange orange

Words with O

Words with P

pen pen pen pen pen pen

stop stop stop stop stop stop

Pig Pig Pig Pig Pig Pig

pie pie pie pie pie pie pie pie

Pear Pear Pear Pear Pear

Words with P

P

P

P

P

P

Words with 2

question question question

Queen Queen Queen Queen

quad quad quad quad quad

equad equad equad equad equad

quiz quiz quiz quiz quiz

Words with 2

z

2

z

e

z

Words with R

Road Road Road Road Road

an an an an an an

miracle miracle miracle

riddle riddle riddle riddle

robot robot robot robot robot

Words with R

R

c

m

n

n

Words with S

soap soap soap soap soap soap

Sheep Sheep Sheep Sheep

star star star star star star

snail snail snail snail snail

muscle muscle muscle

Words with S

Words with T

tiger tiger tiger tiger tiger

Tree Tree Tree Tree Tree

turtle turtle turtle turtle

water water water water water

Team Team Team Team

Words with T

Words with U

Uncle Uncle Uncle Uncle

sun sun sun sun sun

unicorn unicorn unicorn

drum drum drum drum

Uniform Uniform Uniform

Words with U

Words with V

Valentines Valentines

violet violet violet violet

violin violin violin

Velvet Velvet Velvet

venom venom venom venom

Words with V

Words with W

world world world world

Window Window Window

winter winter winter

owr owr owr owr owr owr owr

Worm Worm Worm

Words with W

wa

W

wa

c

W

Words with X

xylophone xylophone

luxe luxe luxe luxe luxe

box box box box box box

taxi taxi taxi taxi taxi taxi

six six six six six six six

Words with X

Words with Y

yellow yellow yellow yellow

Yak Yak Yak Yak Yak

yoghurt yoghurt yoghurt

yoga yoga yoga yoga yoga

gym gym gym gym gym

Words with Y

Words with Z

puzzle puzzle puzzle

lizard lizard lizard lizard

zoo zoo zoo zoo zoo zoo zoo

zombie zombie zombie zombie

Zebra Zebra Zebra Zebra

Words with Z

PART 3

Write sentences in cursive

What to do in Part 3?

- Trace the riddle
- Write again the riddle by yourself
- Try to figure out the challenge and discover the solution in the final pages of the book
- Enjoy it!

Cursive Riddles

Which letter of the alphabet has the most water?

Which letter of the alphabet has the most water?

W

What is black and white and read all over?

What is black and white and read all

over?

W

What kind of room has no door or windows?

What kind of room has no door or windows?

W

What gets bigger the more you get away?

What gets bigger the more you get away?

W

What month of the year has 28 days?

What month of the year has 28 days?

W

What has teeth but can't chew?

What has teeth but can't chew?

W

I go around the world but never leave the corner.
What am I?

I will fill a room but take up no space.
What am I?

I will fill a room but take up no
space.
What am I?
I

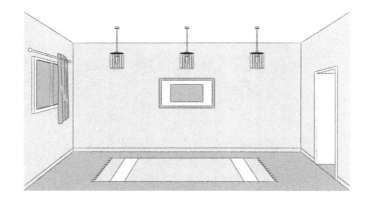

What has to be broken before you can eat it?

What has to be broken before you can eat it?

W

Everyone has one, but no one can lose it.
What is it?

The more of this there is, the less you can see.
What is it?

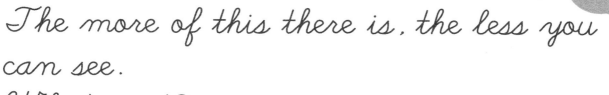

The more of this there is, the less you

can see.

What is it?

Bobby's mother has three children:
Snap, Crackle and . . . ?

Bobby's mother has three children:

Snap, Crackle and . . . ?

B

What has many keys but cannot unlock a single door?

Riddles Solutions

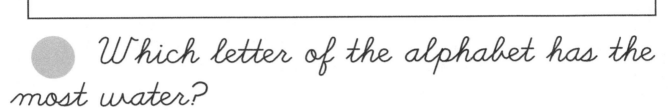

● Which letter of the alphabet has the most water?
The C.

● What is black and white and read all over?
A newspaper.

● What kind of room has no door or windows?
The mushroom.

● What gets bigger the more you get away?
A hole.

● What month of the year has 28 days?
All months have at least 28 days.

What has teeth but can't chew?
A comb.

I go around the world but never leave the corner.
What am I?
A stamp.

I will fill a room but take up no space.
What am I?
The light.

What has to be broken before you can eat it?
An egg.

Everyone has one, but no one can lose it.
What is it?
The shadow.

The more of this there is, the less you can see.
What is it?
Darkness.

Bobby's mother has three children: Snap, Crackle and. . .?
Bobby.

What has many keys but cannot unlock a single door?
A piano.

Made in United States
North Haven, CT
23 March 2025